THE WOMAN WITH A CUBED HEAD

The New Issues Press Poetry Series

Editor   Herbert Scott

Associate Editor   David Dodd Lee

Advisory Editors   Nancy Eimers, Mark Halliday
William Olsen, J. Allyn Rosser

Assistant to the Editor   Rebecca Beech

Assistant Editors   Scott Bade, Allegra Blake, Becky Cooper,
Jeff Greer, Gabrielle Halko, Matthew Hollrah,
Nancy Hall James, Alexander Long,
Tony Spicer, Bonnie Wozniak

Editorial Assistants   Kevin Oberlin, Matthew Plavnick
Diana Valdez

Business Manager   Michele McLaughlin

Fiscal Officer   Marilyn Rowe

The New Issues Press Poetry Series is sponsored by The College
of Arts and Sciences, Western Michigan University, Kalamazoo, Michigan

An Inland Seas Poetry Book

 Inland Seas poetry books are supported by a grant from
The Michigan Council for Arts and Cultural Affairs.

First Edition, 1998.

ISBN: 0-932826-66-0

Library of Congress Cataloging-in-Publication Data:
Moulds, Julie
The Woman with a Cubed Head / Julie Moulds
Library of Congress Catalog Card Number (98-066493)

Art Direction and Design: Tricia Hennessy
Figure Photography: Alfonso Quiroga
Untitled, photograph, 10" x 10", gelatin silver print
Production: Paul Sizer
The Design Center, Department of Art
College of Fine Arts
Western Michigan University
Printing: Bookcrafters, Chelsea, Michigan

THE **WOMAN** WITH A
CUBED HEAD

JULIE MOULDS

New Issues Press

WESTERN MICHIGAN UNIVERSITY

For my Mother and Father
For Larry Syndergaard
And for John

Contents

I

II

III

IV

Acknowledgments

Grateful acknowledgement is made to the journals and anthologies where the following poems first appeared:

Architrave: "Renoir's Bathers"

Christianity and the Arts: "Mary Considers the Geometry of Spheres"

Cream City Review: "Interlochen" and "Choice; or, After Adam Visits a Cathedral to Study a Fresco of Paradise, He Sits in a Pew to Stare at the Ceiling"

Easyriders (Foxyriders): "Iva Drunk with Steel-toed Boots on"

Gulf Coast: "Playing Catch," "When Bad Angels Love Women" and "There Was a Soldier, Not a Sparrow Inside the Golden Cage"

Marlboro Review: "The Conversion of Mary Magdalene"

Mediphors: "One Hundred and Ten Days"

New Millennium Writings: "Bone Marrow Unit: Tracy"

New York Quarterly: "Ghost"

Passages North: "Plucked Eyes"

The PrePress Awards Volume Two: Michigan Voices: "The Dog Poems"

Quarterly West: "Queen Mayadevi, Mother of Buddha, and Mary, Mother of Jesus, Talk About the Clouds"

Quick Brown Fox: "Wedding Iva"

Worcester Review: "The Fish Poem"

I would like to thank PEN American for its generous support, and Lee Dmitzak, Jack Ridl, Nancy Nichodemis, and Bill Olsen for their help and encouragement. Blessings on Beth Amidon, Karen Goebel, Rebecca Markus, and Ruth Barrett—women of power all; and to Melinda, Jenny and Jennifer. Love also to my brother Tony, my sisters Brenda and Sue; and to Armstrong and Saurer, my best men.

I

The Woman with a Cubed Head

There was a young person of Ayr,
Whose head was remarkably square:
On the top, in fine weather, she wore a gold feather;
Which dazzled the people of Ayr.
—Edward Lear, *More Nonsense*, 1877

The woman with a cubed head wears a brilliant gold feather
and two bows where the planes of her head meet.

On the X-ray table, I lie on my side, hands folded.
As the X-rays flash, I fill with questions: what kind

of mating produces a cubed girl? Did her laboring
mother open like an ice machine? And did young Pablo

own a boyhood copy of Lear's *Nonsense*, reading limericks
in Spanish translation? Was Edward actually the father

of the Cubist revolution and Picasso a mere thief?
Or should the questions loom larger: the whys

of tomato-sized tumors; the reasons lungs become
spotted as Dalmatians? The woman is tall, and perhaps

for that her two bedazzled suitors refuse her offered hand—
men have always feared the Amazon. Or perhaps the two

are frightened by her skull's perfect geometry.
Whatever their reason, the suitors still yearn

to dance, and notice she is handsome in apparel:
her dress ornately bordered in triangles, her collar

scalloped like a cloud, her breasts as round as a lax W.
Pablo's three musicians, their cubed heads less perfect

than Lear's, continue to play a comic waltz. Garbed
in Learian harlequin and ruff, and presenting the odd

melodic, the trio further proves there is a Cubist
conspiracy. The brown musician, with his death cloak

and square blue eyes, has been in my hospital room,
his hangman's rope looping over Donna's neck, his blue

heart pulsing cold. He plays a tune with five short beats,
over and over, discordant with the click and release

of the chemo's I.V. drip—a quarter and dotted half note
in monotonous twelve hour song. What inspired Lear

to make his woman's arms and breasts so supple,
but her head so geometric? Remarkable and dazzling,

a beauty with umbrella raised high, why does she offer
hands in peace to those who will refuse them? I have wanted

life at right angles, heads stacked like building blocks,
flat face on flat face. I have wanted to think in crystals,

to have the millennia of a stalactite in the making: the dripping
of liquid over time, the wet minerals coalescing. The idea

already born, L. Frank Baum of Oz knew of Cubism
when his dog, the Woozy, appeared in 1912. Squared body

and ears, cigarette lighter eyes, the Woozy toothlessly
imbibed hives of honeybees. He was fur-less except

for three hairs on his tail, and in Baum's story, a boy
in shaggy blue needed all three for a spell. The Woozy

was loath to part with them. *They are my sole ornament*,
he explained to the crowd assembled: the blue boy,

the Patchwork Girl, the vain glass cat with her rolling
pink brains. The hospital women roll around the aisles,

pink-skulled and pearl-headed. Without eyebrow, nose,
or pubic hair, we are fit for any gallery of grotesques:

our brains glowing in CAT scans, our bodies colonized
by the strange, our hands as blue as Picasso's.

9

On Trumpets and Riddles

I ring with a great noise, because no inner parts weaken
my voice, and breath and winds rule my entire body.
                    from *On the Trumpet*, a medieval riddle

I wish to be beautiful as a riddle: *a whole piece of silk*
that cannot be rolled; ten thousand pearls that cannot

be strung. When I am not beautiful, riddles show me why.
I imagine being so seamless I am simple casement

and funnel: nothing inside like guts or brain, no fear
like cobras crawling through my inner parts. If fire

were a man, he'd have a furnace for lungs. You could open
his hinged doors and throw in emeralds or pine cones,

whatever he craved that day. You could sit in an armchair
and knit while you conversed with fire; while his lungs

warmed you; while the gemstones and knotholes burned.
As long as you were always gathering, he would breathe

forever. And I have met those ruled by breath and wind.
Sometimes I think, if I were truly beautiful, I would keep

the Seventh Commandment; I would not steal. But if stars
can be pearls on lazuli silk, or luminous heifers around

a cowish mother moon, why can't my poetry shake the seeds
of thievery like a rattle in your face? A rattle on a snake

quaking in the sand? Riddlers have considered fire
a golden lizard, a flood of blood, a waving lady's yellow veil.

I want to hide my pink body in a bone cage of riddles;
to deceive Hansel's witch with my offered bone finger.

Can poetry be seamless as water? A voice without bones
or skin? Despite the three regrets, the three withouts,

the three empty things, a trio of my pink selves is soaking
in pine water troughs, being licked by three horses.

The Finnish tell the story that iron once flowed as grey milk
from a maiden's breasts. Then it moved like a snake,

and it hid in a swamp. Is this a last riddle? No,
but the horses have always wondered about that story.

Perhaps they have tasted the breasts of my submerged
women, have drawn in milky iron or fire;

or perhaps they would rather drink in pure water
than suckle pink melons that swell with the moon.

When Bad Angels Love Women

When the bad angel loves
the woman next door,
the motion wakes me.
The tip of one of his
purple-veined wings
moves right through our walls.
It lifts and falls
as the two of them, a wind
like blue leather pulsing
through this house.
She packs cartons
of eggs like I do, during days,
with other women and boys
on a line. But home,
there is this angel.
His kiss, like a scorpion's,
marks her now, and suddenly
I have seen her tilting
out of time. When her
night voice winds
like a blue leather wind,
I know he is there.
She goes to him now
and he eats her
like a young apple,
the way men eat a woman
in a dark alley
until she is gone.
One day, he is with her always
his windy presence
rolling the eggs
from our cartons.
The ladies and I are tired

of all this breaking;
tired of seeing dollar-sized
bites disappear
from her neck. She
is the color of blueberries
on cheesecloth.
Antlers or the bones
of wings break her back.
Luminescent, like blue neon,
she tries to fill her cartons,
but the eggs
slip through her hands.
I could hear him each night
eat her soul,
I say to the ladies on the line
the day she disappears.
The whole house could hear
while we stacked
our wet plates,
his giant wings spreading
like a fan.

The Mary Ballads

(after the Finnish *Kanteletar*)

The curtains open to a puppet Virgin
on my hand. Mary bows to a Star, says,

Have you seen Jesus, who made
my womb hard?

The Star says, *I am angry*
with Jesus. He made me to stay always

in night and cold; to float like dust
in a dark meat locker.

The Virgin turns to the Moon,
asks again,

Have you seen Jesus? Have you seen my bundle
from heaven?

The Moon complains in a moon voice,
I am angry with Jesus, His cruel

gifts: the shrink and shiver and grow.
Mary whirls her lace dress

for the moonlight, but the Moon
won't tell Mary anything.

Third, the Virgin greets the Sun: a golden
wheel cogged in light.

When Mary asks, *Where is my boy?*
Where is my womb berry?

the Sun, like a megaphone,
announces, *Jesus is dead*

and trapped under rocks. Mary makes
the Sun melt the rocks.

Orange coal Jesus, ready to rise,
the Virgin whirls

her lace dress in sunlight. Jesus is pulled
to heaven with strings.

Late Summer Litany

My neighbor's almost ex-husband, an auto salesman with a
different car each week, is over to visit his son, a lively bear cub
of a boy. The man only comes over with electric prodding, to his
son's delight. In the former's defense, the man cannot help that
he enjoys golf more than small boys. His two daughters from
another marriage live in Maine and do not demand much of him.
He says marriage has bit him in the ass two times and he has
learned his lesson. My neighbor upstairs grieves, as anyone
would, at their failure. She remembers the charm he had ten
percent of the time. I sit on my concrete steps, drinking cold rum,
watching the boy enter another new car. The crickets and the
birds keep repeating, *we don't change, we don't change*, and the
fireflies turn on and off like love.

Interlochen

A motorcycle idles, and from its exhaust
I rise, choking on black smoke from a piece

of wood in the biggest bonfire I've ever seen,
the one Dave Marlatt had to get a permit for: fire,

like an oboe crescendo; fire, like the young *artistes*
holding hands and igniting themselves; fire,

like the wall socket, more alive than the tragicom
pair of faces on our wall. The cottage curtains

collect the virginities of the young girls
in blue uniforms, as the great Virgin looks down

disgusted at all the hymens broken here.
And despite our great efforts, Mary, garbed today

in patchwork, again blesses my womb with barrenness.
She ignores the more popular terms: uterus, sterility,

sperm count. She does not acknowledge that penis
means tail in Greek. And pulling that tail farther,

what do we need, in this life, to infuse it? Did all
those transfusions I had in the hospital help? The red

corpuscles, the clarified plasma of other people?
I read in a murder mystery how the killer

had a bone marrow transplant and nearly escaped
his brutality, because his DNA had changed.

It no longer matched that of his earlier crime.
And how every two years our bodies completely

regenerate themselves. In this hot plate universe,
in this hierarchy of artists, what place is there for me,

the last chair flutes scrambling up each other's backs
like rats, their hallelujahs rising from their silver pipes?

A woman sews in her cabin window and I remember
Baba Yaga, whose underground tailors stitched up soldiers

for her fight against that great skeleton, Kolchey.
Like marionettes without masters, those sewn fighters

rose to their slaughter. But then again, if a person's
not really alive, perhaps it's acceptable to kill him.

Maybe we can always re-piece ourselves, like the great boar
in Valhalla, who could feed ten thousand Vikings,

and regrow flesh in the morning if his bones
were carefully placed back together.

Soup Bone

I am running to the butcher shop for a soup bone.
—Carl Sandburg, *Rootabaga Stories*

You'd think the cardboard in his shoes
would come loose, the way those ankles
fly down the road. The boy passes

a girl pounding the round lid
of a coffee can with a stick.
The boy's father, though a wainwright,

isn't really much more than a careless man
mounting his favorite
girl for hire. He drives her down

the same time the boiling begins,
the same moment the boy returns
and the mother slivers cabbage

into the soup pot and opens
the white wax package. The mother's
knife gleams, and she's singing. The boy

makes hand prints with blood
from the bone's white wrapping
on the back of a yellow dog.

The father, now walking home,
whistles in the ways
of those who enjoy sin and pardon,

while the little girl's hands
tap a pattern on her coffee tin,
and she plays it, over and over.

19

Mary Considers the Geometry of Spheres—

That the circumference of a woman nine months
along is caused by the additions of chromosome
x plus x or x plus y. Even God, when He planted

His seed, followed this rule. The area of Mary
carrying Christ, like the area of a sphere,
is the squared radius of the moon, times the infinite

trail of numbers behind that three, beyond *pi*,
tempting us like the apple down a road
as far as we are out of Eden. It's always the three,

and then some, like the Holy Trinity and Mary;
Mary, a long blue ribbon wrapped around Father,
Son, and Spirit. Inexact, and hard to define,

but part of the equation.

The Girl Listens to the Crooning of the Danish Balladeers

In a forest world where women pick lice from their killer's hair,
or Island Losa defends her honor against sixty men, then walks

away in bloody shoes; from that land where the dead lover
comes back to his dear Elsey, carrying a wooden coffin

on his back; from there I am exiled. This is my life: blue carpet,
four walls; books, not children; an alliance, not husband.

Stevenson said come down off this feather-bed of civilization—
feel the globe granite underfoot. But I'm afraid to leave here,

afraid of the green, afraid of my body growing round.
Even dead Sir Ogey, the coffin carrier, wanted his own true love

to move on. As wished Sweet Willy's ghost to his Margret.
Both women withered anyway, like fragile magnolias or roses.

My lover is a weed. No, I am a weed: ugly and rooted
in this manicured lawn. Not even in a wild meadow

to be fucked by bees or butterflies. My lover is some beautiful
germ swimming in water. Quick. Unstable. Mating in words

and body with other women, men, stable hands, horses, anything
that moves. His love is quick and real and cheap

and easily memorialized. It seems the Norse understood cruelty:
like Volund Smith, who, after killing the king's sons,

coated their skulls with silver so the boys could cradle
their father's wine, be tendered by his lips; or Fenja and Menja,

the chained Giant women, who turned (like the cuckoo's song)
the Peace Mill, until, disgusted, they helped it all go up

in flames. I, too, know the slavery of peace. The need
to go to Newfoundland, make my own story, my old story
unwilling to come along.

Atlas in Space

His bony arms can't hold up the sky. Don't be fooled by the talk
that his biceps roll like a squad of tanks up his shoulders;

or that the tattoos of a hundred blue whales swim nightly
across his back. Atlas commissioned Vulcan to forge a machine

replacing his hands and shoulders. Now he can sit
for spells of a century, before sprockets start squeaking for oil.

His thirteen league legs have grown thin, and his torso
now sags to a belly blown bigger than a planet. What else

has he to do? His mouth, a black hole, he swallows the rocks
and satellites that fly through the universe. He, like most men,

had children to bear: the Pleiades, who burst like white pigeons
into space; the Hyades, those rainy stars, who nursed

and nannied Bacchus. His wife, Aethra, once a princess
of the sea, whispers and curls with him on dark nights,

in the conch-like twists of his ear.

Renoir's Bathers

What is it about women in water
that almost makes them part of the landscape?
Renoir's bathers, pink and mustard
and vaguely nippled; their ample thighs
rising from a purple river in a scene
centered by one brown tree. What is it
about women, painted by men,
that they become landscapes, creamy roses
in a garden? In another age,
when people could still sleep
with almost anyone, my sister and I dipped
ourselves naked in a Michigan lake, both of us,
still, miraculously, virgins.
I suppose some painter in that art colony
where Brenda washed dishes
could have captured us, like Renoir,
two flowers with leafy thighs and brown
daisy faces. Perhaps he would accent
our round hymens with petals. I want to be
the woman, with her brush, sitting in an oak
above a pond where twelve nude men are frolicking.
She is painting a landscape of men:
lying flat with grapes above their open mouths;
men, with buttocks turned towards her; men,
with arms arched behind their long necks.
She would call it *The Dozen Adonae*. Pink
chrysanthemum men; dark, magnolia men;
legs spread, organs rising or fallen,
depending on your eyes. In another time,
in a deserted field, I lay naked as a lover
wrapped me in oil. I must have even walked
through high grass, and, knowing me, worried
about where bugs could enter.

Insects never crawl up the legs
in the paintings of the three Graces.
In those landscapes of the masculine
dream, men want to paint us perfect,
from a distance, then break petals,
like a cloud or a swan.

Variations on My Room in the Bone Marrow Unit:
In the Room of Scissors

Scissors, every pair I ever used, hanging from penny nails
on walls, hanging like silver chromosomes
on colored yarn from the ceiling; blades built into the floor

like that iron bed of proverbs. The scissors are bright
preschool plastic; tiny toenail; jagged pinking shears
I loved from mother's sewing box; left-handed scissors

that never worked in elementary. They are the barber's shears
used to cut my hair that didn't fall, the second time
my hair let go. The barber stays with me in my room,

though he sits as far away as he can. I walk over, offer
him my last remnants of curls, say, *I've never gone
to a barber before*. He answers, *It's not like going to the moon*,

and speaks nothing more to me, even after clipping
off my little mohawk and my final stubborn pair of tufts.
He gets his money and my hair never grows back.

My head is lunar and I start to wear his spare green barber coat
but he still won't talk, so I change to blue hospital robes, walk
through the shop, avoiding the floor blades. The clippers buzz

and roar, beckoning customers to come. The music makes
the scissors leap from their nails and dance on the long
shop counter, kicking up sharp chromed legs.

The barber, a businessman, charges his clients double
to watch, his patients a line of bruise-eyed women
and men, their mouths sewn shut with catgut.

They enter with fuzz on their heads and leave smooth as stones.
Everyone exits, but I can't, and stare through the glass
at the door locked from the outside; stare at the clock

saying when the barber will return. The scissors and I
are alone. I hate the barber, but anything chrome
behaves when he is here. Now they are scissors

with an agenda: I am disease, a Gulliver-sized pogrom,
a ritual purification to make happen. Not being threaded
needles, can they cut out the bad and not leave me

to bleed? lymph nodes, ovaries, lungs? The scissors
walk towards me like little John Waynes, and I focus
on the clock, play with its red plastic hands.

Even the hands are scissors.

II

Rapture Three

I

I never did anything dangerous as a child, except to fall
down the stairs, arms back, trying to fly. I never jumped
off roofs or dangled from rafters in an unfinished garage.
I was the girl who read library books on the playground
by the diamond linked fence, who only got asked
to jump rope when the other girls wanted someone
to turn the yellow plastic handle . . . When the phone rings
on this Friday night, it's a drunk friend of my husband's.
I answer, pretending I'm asleep because I'd rather not talk
to lonely alcoholics who call every weekend. Half my relatives
died from riding their snowmobiles too many times
to the bars all winter in the Upper Peninsula,
and my Italian mother reminds me that alcoholism is genetic
on my father's side. I'm lonely too, and wanted that voice
on the phone to be my husband's, in Detroit, on a crew
building an International House of Pancakes. It is just after
the third time they've found cancer, and I'm unwilling to leap
right back into the fight. I will have to soon enough: shots,
radiation, chemo; exercise, vitamins, visualization—
there's no point rushing the inevitable. The news is new,
and I deserve a chance to enjoy my hair awhile.
The local doctor whom I just ditched, first told me
of only two tumors, though he knew of four, and before
my biopsy, I told my friend, *Don't worry, I'm ninety-nine
per cent perfect*, but there's more colonies of those bad cells
than even the doctor realized, and each one
might as well be a stop sign inside my heart, my abdomen,
my ovaries; scarlet sickle Cs cutting off my decades as
the CAT scanner looks for more with its radiating eyes.

II

As a child, I read through Andrew Lang's entire series
of folk tales, hue by hue: the *Violet Fairy Book*, the *Grey*,
the *Crimson*. And though I don't remember the stories—
except the one about the talking horse head on the barn wall
who advised the local shepherd girl—I still remember
where the volumes were shelved, to the right of the window
by the church where I attended Girl Scouts. Fairy tales all
have the same plot anyway, a boy-girl fighting a witch-ogre-troll,
and we either survive or are eaten. Today I told a woman
who didn't ask, I have no intention of dying soon.
The woman in expensive silver jewelry was just saying sorry
to hear I needed chemo again, having just watched
her mother go through it. What can they do to me they haven't
already? The chemo and shots and bone marrow transplant.
I think maybe this time I won't beat it back.
But I can't think that. Tonight I met a children's writer,
who read aloud her latest picture book. I thought
of my own manuscripts; and of my own children
who likely won't exist. My picture books remain safe
at home in a box, but I morbidly think of my other
library treasures, and doubt anyone else will love them:
Memoirs of a Tattooist; *Legends of the Bells*; and my 1930s
facsimile editions of *Babar*. I want to sleep, but I'm waiting
for my call, and can't stop thinking about my visit

to the oncologist today, the doctor who suggested I just let
the cancer spread since my marrow transplant had failed.

III

I pick up from the nurse my files and biopsy slides,
and in the next room, the chemo room, there's a man
in an easy chair, legs up, as if watching a Michigan
football game, and he's smiling. He looks a lot like my doctor,
and I have to glance again to see the I.V. bag dripping
into him. And maybe my mind put the doctor in that chair,
so the infusion would make him understand more
about being diseased than he does. What do you do
about something unwanted, like a tumor or a phone call
that keeps repeating? I consider having a portrait taken
of me while I still have hair or buying six African hats.
I think of triple-piercing my ears, and purchasing polish
to paint my nails in green and magenta. But my adventures
should be bigger than what I can accomplish in three hours
at a mall. I should think constellations and transcendence
and becoming sunlight. My mother, a child of the fifties,
always wears red lipstick. There's something exotic about that,
something that would require a bit of courage. My husband
called at midnight, while I was undressing. I almost said,
teasingly, *I'm half naked right now*, when his drunken brother,
uninvited, picked up the line and started to listen.
I felt violated and angry that he would intrude, even though
I hadn't said anything a brother couldn't hear. I thought again,
I hate drunks: people who've chosen to be sick
and tell crude jokes at family dinners, turning into monsters
who come at you with knives, or fall asleep in cars
with the motors running. My stomach filled with acid, and I
wanted to hang up on my husband to make that second voice
go away. When the nurse is about to hook me up
for chemotherapy, it feels like that. Fear that something
dehumanizing or invasive or deadly is about to happen.
Then the chemicals enter, and the anti-nauseas dope me up,
and it's another day when life's not bad if I'm in survival mode.

33

IV

I panicked, started to shake, right before my last biopsy,
done on a CAT scan table. The doctor ran me through
the machine then drew a line with black marker above
my tumor for the needle. So much depended on the tests
being benign, and I didn't want to go back to that unslept in
hospital bed, my bags not yet unpacked, for five more years.
That terror is what I feel now, but I'm in my own sheets,
alone, having received the voices of two drunk men
and my husband tonight. Now the telephone ringer is off
and I'm in double-layered sweats because this house is cold.
The window behind me is cracked, and sometimes I can smell
the neighbor's cigarette when he smokes outside
before leaving for his third shift job. I've seen them huddled
at the back entrance of the hospital, the skinny men
and women with their rolling I.V.'s, smoking outside
in their bedclothes, despite everything. And I know cigarettes
might have brought them there, but I admire the tenacity
of those patients, to go out in their robes, blowing out
white smoke and breath, when most in that place
don't even leave their beds. And whatever I said earlier
about drunks, there's something sad about a life
without vices, which is why I won't quit coffee. Today
in the oncology office I saw that man grinning in an easy chair,
being dripped into, and I no longer felt separate as I have
for three years. Tonight I sit in the recliner with him
as the ceiling drizzles down a chemical rain and the man's
smiling head nuzzles my ear like the slurry voices
of alcoholics I've hung up on.

V

I can't sleep, and go into the barn to ask advice
of the talking horse. Will he prescribe the ten dollar cures?
Burdock root? Red clover? Green tea? Can he get me,
on the black market, that new lymphoma drug
concocted from Mammoth Cave fungus and the antibodies
of a mouse? I should have worn a costume
because I'm not the shepherd girl, and the horse
won't talk to me. He blinks, but then stares
with the same sandy eyes as a mounted buck in a tavern.
I remember, when young, I was convinced I would fly,
if only I could master the technique. I gathered
the house's bed pillows, spread them through the living room,
got a running start then leapt, and leapt. I practiced for hours,
not losing hope, while my mother with her red lips
never said a word: the carpet soft, the furniture cleared,
and nothing valuable in that room but me. It's odd,
when you're in peril, the adrenaline quickens. And before
the terror, like the pilot in the cockpit of an open biplane,
there's the joy of wind and danger and not being dead
that people pay to die for on Mount Everest. All week,
friends have been sending me presents, as if it were
my birthday. Cancer's like that, if you can survive:
a perilous birth party on a rope bridge.

The Dog Poems

1. Dog Grows Fish Scales

It was after winter shedding he noticed
the first silver. A coat of armor really,
making him look like one of those robot dogs
in science fiction movies.

He enjoyed the change.
A silver dog shimmers in the moonlight
and is never ignored at dance halls.

Dog wonders about this phenomenon—
will he grow gills? Are there furry fish?
When he swims, will he make
some fisherman become deranged?

In his nightmares, he is being scaled
and deboned, even though he is a dog.
He is sold at the fish counter,
even though he is red meat.

2. If Dog Were a River, What Color Would He Be?

The country bar played
Cry Me a River.
Dog relieved himself outside
like a dog.
He thought of the brown mud puddle he stood in
and the green Schnapps he'd been drinking all night.
He thought of his bitch's menstrual blood
and the yellow piss running down his leg.
These are all good colors for rivers.

3. Leda and the Dog

Forget the white plumage and clever clouds. Dog is Dog.
He knows all women eventually dream of animals:
the pink testicles hidden in fur. This accounts
for the canine boys in the tabloid news,
or the wolf children in jungles and circuses.
Women forget what they might be breeding.

Dog doesn't care. Dog is Dog. Leda was in heat
and Dog can't ignore these things.

4. Clay Dog

The Lord said,
Thou shalt have no false gods before me.

But there was Dog, kneeling before his clay dog,
barking out a prayer.
The idol was a terrier, like Angus,
and God was angry because He was a big god
and didn't like little dogs.

God flashed down to Dog as lightning and said
I am at least a Great Dane,
or a Doberman.
Or, if you prefer kindness, a Collie dog,
but not a Scotty.

Dog was smote with fire. God smote the Scotty too.

5. Dog as Jesus

Except for the crucifixion
Dog didn't mind.

He enjoyed leading, and it was easy to be good
when he tried.

Wisdom? Well, he had speech writers for that.
And Magdalene was always discreet.

The nails hurt Dog's paws.
A dog's body isn't meant to hang straight
and he flailed horribly.

6. Geriatric Dog

His back leg has a permanent gimp.
He has tumors all over his body.
He eats cortisone every day, prescribed by his doctor,
and is on a low cholesterol diet—no more eggs.
His teeth, even after fillings, fall out.

Dog is tired. Cancer eats his body.
His children and grandchildren and great-grandchildren
are all ungrateful. His friends have never been kind.

7. Dog Comes Back as a Puppy

Delightful to be reborn
as a puppy, with the mind of a dog.
He sucks on each of his mother's nine breasts.
He does not think of her as his mother.
Dog grows fast and he looks the same. Dog is Dog.
You can't kill him.

IV

Jonah and Noah

You can't ignore the call of God. Look at Mary and the berry;
Jonah and God's whale. A man, when he is swallowed,

remembers the womb. Jonah, Dove of God, tried to fly away
but ended up in Jehovah's jail. If Mary were a whale

and we were in her belly, could we escape, like Jonah,
with an insincere psalm? Could we be insincere, after singing

of lilies, singing of berries and rosebuds and apples?
The Slavs said the world was supported by four whales,

each cetus stationed at a corner of the sea. When Noah sailed,
the whales left their posts for the journey, choosing to swim

in formation near the ark: Noah was carrying the world
in his boat; Noah was carrying Adam's bones in his hull.

He carried Adam's bones, but left Eve's unburied; left them
to drain in the fields outside Eden; left her old marrow

to be eaten by ants. Jesus as a fish swims next to the Ark.
He knows that from Noah will come the Jews and from the Jews

will come the Christians. As Jesus heeds both these faiths,
He must make sure that Noah survives. Jesus, the fish,

listens as Noah captains his sons. His sons all have names
but not their wives. Things are often that way: A begat B;

B begat C—but what of the bearers? The bearers did their part
but became anonymous. Jesse's rod and all that rot.

Plucked Eyes

He met a young man having but one eye . . .
so Miach put the cat's eye in his head.
　　　　　　　　　—Lady Gregory

In Dublin, while wrens dive from the elders,
the man's left eye follows those rolling brown birds

as they split the sky. Instead of a paw, his hand starts to rise,
swipes at the air like a tabby. And his slant green eye snaps

like a shutter in sun, or his slant green eye twitches
after field mice and bees.

　　　　　　　*

Sometimes the soldier, his right eye asleep,
would creep to a farmhouse, bite into a bird

while it was still breathing—a chick in the hen yard.
The man would awake to himself on his haunches

in dark, in gravel, with a round salty head
all red and all yellow, rolling blood on his tongue;
and a warm puff of body beneath a red palm.

　　　　　　　*

Inside the farm window he saw three German girls
with six eyes amongst them. The First was a Cyclops;

the Second had three eyes, different colors, her last eye
as brown as the knob on a drawer. The girl with two eyes,

still sweet in blue rag, would be knifed by the mother
who could not abide the mundane.

The Conversion of Mary Magdalene

(after a medieval play)

1.
God be with my valentines: And Mary Magdalene
transforms sleeping air in her arbor to sweet,

oily perfume. She has within her all Seven Deadly Sins;
Lechery her sweet leech in yellow silk;

Lechery, her maidservant, who moves her
from the Castle of Magdalene to a Jerusalem brothel

and princely bedmen who fan her with green palms
and say, *ah, open again, my daisy.*

2.
Devils itch where you do, hands in breeches on a wooden stage.
We now present: the Flesh, the World, the Temple.

But if a sinful medieval guildsman with a rope
soaked in wine can tie it behind a soon burgeoning

costumed Virgin; can climb up like God with it to the rafters,
torch it at Gabriel's cue to lead Sweet Jhesu's soul

down like lightning; if even he can light the fire
of the Annunciation, Mary, couldn't you? Counting

His almond toes, marveling that even God has feet
to wrap in hair and oil, like some old valentine?

3.
Mary, to sleep with the Prince of Flesh, was to be covered
with bright flowers; to be given, on every occasion, seeds

of paradise and ginger. Can your woman's hands stop dreaming
of polishing cocks and silver?

Lazarus, regal in robes of riches, you had two houses, you had
two sisters; you're now in a tomb with fine bleached

linen; a mummy in the womb, carried by two sisters.
Jhesu walks slow with oily feet. Sleep, baby sleep.

4.
A woman can wander for four hundred years
and still die, over the desert of a stage, costumed

seraphs singing, *Sweet, Dead Mary.* All your womanly
water and cinnamon traded for thirty years

of clouds and feeding angels. You came out smelling
like a rose, sailing Mary, and your bones didn't even end.

There Was a Soldier, Not a Sparrow, Inside the Golden Cage

(after a Russian tale)

Disguised as a sparrow, he watched
Princess Emma unbraid yellow hair,

saw petticoats falling, corsets unlacing,
as he sang her ditties he'd heard in the fields.

She thought the brown bird had come from some suitor;
the old woman said so—the girl took her word.

Four servants were needed to bring in his birdhouse.
(The hag, on her horse cart, left town.)

My little brown songster, my sweet
feathered warbler, who sent you to sing?

crooned Emma, who circled the cage in her bloomers
while the dressmaker laced her all in.

To see Emma close, he had wandered the forest,
cornered a hag to conjure a cage.

The hag, who was partial to those with brass buttons,
pulled him up close, then feathered him, small;

said he could unlatch his cage during slumbers
of golden-haired girls between brocade drapes.

Could switch, with a wish, his feathers for skin.
(Now back to the princess.) The girl took him in.

Imagine the girl's rage, to wake, him above her.
She raised up her mirror, cracked open his crown;

yelled for her lady, then saw in his falling
not a man, but a bird, come down.

The cage door ajar, the girl understood
that soldier and sparrow were always the same.

The nurse swept the mirror, the girl wrapped the sparrow
up tight in her stocking. His little head glistened.
His lungs folded in.

Ghost

Even in the seventeenth century, you couldn't get away
with slicing your wife in two. He thought

she'd been unfaithful, and why not, men and women
always are, but while her head and torso began to haunt

the rooms near the cubbyhole he'd stoned her corpse into,
her skirted lower half still chastely glided through

the churchyard, as if to say *maybe my mouth kissed*
a few lords in the barn, but I kept that wifely part pure for you.

It was a clean division—no blood—like that of magicians'
assistants, their feet kicking, hands waving; the space

between their divided coffins like that between God
and Adam. Her body was parted but uncorrupt, like a martyr's,

his dicing more than making up for her few indiscretions.
People began to get suspicious when the young wife

he'd claimed was taken by French fever started appearing,
bottomless, to his house guests; began to burn her lips

onto their sleeping faces, to spite him. One could speak
of the separation of intellect and flesh, the flesh personified

by her floating, silk-covered cunt, but that doesn't work here:
the cavern of the mouth is so close to the brain stem,

and the brain is always still thinking of the kiss.
After he was discovered, her two halves leading the searchers

to the corpse, the man became strangely absent
from his stronghold; while her cloven immortality

has lingered there for three hundred years, like the violet
perfume he poured over her parts. Her bottom does its odd,

leggy dance on the carpets. Her top bangs the clavichord,
and does simple fractions on the walls with coal. The men

she kisses always look down, expecting, as with other women,
to see her skirt-covered other mouth below.

Choice; or, After Adam Visits a Cathedral to Study a Fresco of Paradise, He Sits in a Pew to Stare at the Ceiling

Adam, a white soul, after all his spinning through thistle, sweat,
sweet evil and exile, enters, like muslin, God's house.

He watches the ceiling; groined vaults, zigzagged ribs:
how each painted part rises and falls, meets and merges,

like the pieces of men, or the sweet, gold, breathing
body of God. He, like His house, is held together

with ribs, and Adam, clay or man or spirit made white,
wonders which rib in this body of God

is choice; is woman; the bloodied bone God held
like a divining rod; water for His fruit; fire

for His fields; the opposite of one;
the wish for something other

than light. Beneath the gilded ceiling, Adam sings
for his lady, made by God's hand. He remembers

her green voice, the green garden, and God,
crossing His song with hers; the harmony, the fire.

Queen Mayadevi, Mother of Buddha
and Mary, Mother of Jesus, Talk About the Clouds

The women agree. When mortals draw a cloud,
most depict the cumulus, a scalloped, oblong doily.

The average child with crayons is ignorant of delicate
cirrus, turreted castellanus, ragged nimbostratus.

The women can't agree who's the greater, the container
or the contained; or what the earthly role should be

for women who are cosmic wombs. Though their faces
are placid in paintings, the two sit high on a mother cloud

and argue. All mothers can talk of gestation, and Mayadevi
reveals she held Buddha within her like a cloud

holds a lightning bolt, and how it hurt to have such heat
in a belly. Mary confides that statues of her are too often

hollow; she wishes to become a porcelain body,
bigger than the world, so she might float within her

every human soul, each one writhing and red as a babe;
the congregation filling her inner space like balloons in a sky.

The women's voices drift to the beauty of clouds:
white-veiled cirrostratus, modestly heralding celestial storms;

shadowless cirrocumulus, its buxom mamma dripping
down as do mothers for sons. Mary loves best

altocumulus, with its virga, mamma, coronae, and haloes.
She spends days in its humid form, baptizing the virgins

without umbrellas, washing out the open mouths
of blasphemers, crowning her cathedrals in violet,

and circling over the lonely, who read adventures on park
benches. Though the Indians have equally valid terms

for clouds, Mayadevi has made a lullaby of the Latin ones.
In varied repetitions, she chants *cirrus* for bird's tuft,

incus for anvil, *pannus* for the ascetic's tatters of cloth.
Whenever clouds are in the crosswords, the women

can fill in the squares. They like word games and mystery
novels. They are proud of their accomplished sons,

but would have preferred a world without nails and bad pork.

Three Iva Poems

1. Iva Drunk with Steel-toed Boots on

didn't have to borrow
her uncle's Harley.
She had her own—deep red
as a whore's lipstick.
She roared to the bar,
black chaps over Levi's.
Eagle wings patched
her scrawny behind.
A leather laced halter
fringed her belly,
exposing a small rose tattoo.
Iva hadn't drunk enough
to pose for *Easyriders*; she
would surely try.

2. The Fish Poem

Iva looked at the clear fishline, the canned
beer on ice. *You'll like this*, he said.
There's peace in this warm sun.
I'll teach you to cast and reel . . . Iva wanted
to be on the water. To be the pheasant
feather fly a brook trout would die for.
To wiggle into that pink mouth,
and whisper, wicked, *It is too late.*
You should not have swallowed,
while the line pulls his gills into air.

3. Wedding Iva

Stars shot gold
over evening mass—
she planned the wedding
so the sky gave blessing;
married a man
no one had seen.
(His face appeared
when *I do's* began,
rose as the stone
in her ring.)

In their wedding room
she read
from *Modern Dimensions
of Heroic Life*.
He licked her ribs
till she softened.
She nibbled his neck
like a mushroom stem.
When he held her
she became
white and armless
like a goddess
or a bowling pin.

After Lunch in the Bar with John Armstrong

I am free of babies, my breasts
shrinking from little mouths, my belly as flat
as any virgin's.

> *A nursing dancer squirts her milk*
> *to the paying men offstage,*
> *a thin, human cream.*

Today, I offend a man by saying his writing
is not good. What it needs, I think, is more blood;
blood, like when I cut you
shaving your wet, angled face.

> *Hot iron pocks our fathers' faces*
> *in my hometown steelyard;*
> *the unprotected heads nearly boil*
> *above vats of tomato-red heat.*

I have read others' letters.
How the two recline
into each other:

> *His tongue drops down like a fish*
> *into her mouth. He loves*
> *pink breasts and yellow leaves.*

It is easy to live for lying in bed
wrapped around a man-sized child.
Hemingway's doctor, last ditch, gave an Indian girl
a Caesarean, without anesthesia.

The father, in the bunk
above her screams,
slits his throat.

As a child, I collected stories of severed heads,
like victorious Judith, swinging the general's beard
before the Jews.

And Orpheus, too true to love
other men's wives; his wet, singing head
bobbing down some Nile.

Bone Marrow Unit: Tracy

I knew a man who left his wife after nine years of chemo—
left her to die, her lungs filling like someone underwater.
In my mind, she is drowning still and forever;
gasping and making bad jokes, like the last time we talked.
She was funny, I tell my husband, *feisty-funny*
with a little acid laced in. Tracy, I imagine
that other husband stating, *I want children, and a wife*
who isn't rotting, and, yes, I've picked her already.
And that, I know, approaches the truth.
Whatever he said, he said it long distance,
over the phone, out east from Maine or Maryland.
He tells her he's left while she's Intensive Care,
a hygienic room in a bone marrow unit in Illinois.
A week later that woman—with whom I'd laughed and walked,
other months and this, before
they siphoned the bone marrow from my blood—
a week later that woman was dead. I was asleep or drugged
and connected to six machines, but Tracy
was up that night, screaming in the tide. My husband,
wandering the halls in his yellow scrubs, paper hat,
and blue boots had to hear, until morning, more death
than he wanted to, with me three doors away.
She was my age, thirty-two, and still
honeymooning in Florida when her cancer came.
We used to like to play tennis, she said.
Her husband had gall to fly in that last morning.
Had gall to make that final appearance. I tell myself
not to judge: only God can do that. Tracy had been
through more chemotherapy than anyone I ever knew—
and maybe this was the only way God could get her to die.

Playing Catch

There was an old person of Minety
Who purchased five hundred and ninety
Large apples and pears, which he threw unawares,
At the heads of the people of Minety.
                    —Edward Lear, *More Nonsense*

If you are big enough, I suppose anything can be thrown:
circus strong men, elephants, fat ladies. The trick is to grow

larger than anyone else, like Menja, the Norse jewel-maid
who rose through her girlhood tossing truck-size boulders.

The great nonsense painter, Edward Lear, in numerous
journeys through remote terrain, often had to dodge rocks

while sketching. Those nineteenth century natives of Albania
and Greece would yell, *Scroo, Scroo!* and *Devil, he draws!*

as Lear exoticized their turbans for his posh Anglo patrons.
Edward had probably broken some taboo in each attempt

to replicate a human spirit; and spirits, having mouths
and hands, often choose to pelt a captor. A boy coughs

as he passes the house on bicycle, and that sound travels
and spins through the screen, proving we are always throwing

something: plates, fits, fists. Even heads, back to the killers
who severed them—back and forth and back, the slain man's

daughter saying, *I don't want my father's head. Don't want to*
carve daddy's head up for dinner. And motherless Lear,

old Victorian, had a heart that pitched quite improperly
against the walls he decided to obey. Perhaps this explains

his travel to climates so far from the gentlemen he craved.
His heart would say, if he'd let it, *We need love and love*

and love in this life, in a steady dose of capture and toss,
and his limerick man fulfilled half that equation:

throwing his affection at the heads of the people he lived for.
And if they didn't throw it back, apple or pear, perhaps

they bit in. A woman, grieving, said to her open-casket mother,
You did not teach me happiness. You did not teach me happiness.

And maybe we can learn it, like the rules of any game with balls.
This is the proper stance. That is where you hold your hands.

Muskegon

The walnuts fall fluorescent green and we kick
them inside our arches like soccer balls
down the sidewalk. I gather the nuts from the street,
save the ones that will get run over by cars
or swept up by the City, throw them in the woods
by the cornfield. This weekend I traveled home
to a wedding reception at the Sons of Norway Hall.
The groom, in handcuffs, crawled under his bride's dress,
grabbed her garter with his teeth. Mothers dragged
their bright daughters from the room; my young nephews,
both in tuxedo shoes, kept staring at their shiny feet.
The next day, we attended the funeral of an ex-cousin.
He had died at eighty in a risky cancer operation,
choosing that instead of wasting away in a home.
He was old, at least, I say about anyone who dies
late of the disease; not young like me or the ten year olds.
My grandmother, in her Depression house on the hill,
with the willow we swung from, and the field
our relatives sent us snipe hunting in—my grandmother
showed us pictures of children, now middle-aged or dead:
Uncle Sam in spurs. Epileptic Aunt Terry, smiling big,
holding the gifts my homesick father sent her from Germany.
And dozens of pictures of my grandfather
holding babies. The topic changes to who is smoking
too much, and someone asks about my *lymphomia*,
pronouncing it like *symphonia*, and I want to laugh,
like the girl at the gas station, who saw the sign:
Need a penny? Take a penny, and changed the verse
to *Need a tumor? Take a tumor*. At Sunday Mass,
I pause at the lines asking forgiveness
for what I have done, and what I have failed to do—
part of a weekly Catholic creed going back to Nicea.
I know *what we fail to do* is always the most damning.

His arms rising up, there's a new Jesus
on the Crucifix, in white robes, instead of a loincloth—
not the usual corpse on the wall. If I've become
numb to His death, I also resent this happy Savior,
think of my college churches—not one candle, not one
Christ painted with bloody hands. The Prophet Isaiah,
whom I've always thought of as a poet, tells
of the vengeful vineyard owner who commands
the clouds not to rain on his grapes, but my mother's
not that way. All weekend, she feeds me from her pantry;
lets me wash linens in her machines. We fold clothes,
and I remember my brother saying
that he'd raked his lawn in terror the day his wife
and newborn came home from the hospital.
The two were asleep as he picked up the leaves,
thinking, *How do I care for something so small?*
How do we know what to do?

After Reading Rumi

I say my prayers upside down, the wind
blowing me like a clothespinned robe,
my little bat hands curled together. I look for God

in a school of fish. I look for God in Mammoth Cave.
I look for God in an air balloon. If Jesus'
hot coal head is the sun rising, where does

He hide his body? Or does the body merely
flatten black like a shadow, then disappear in sun?
An unravelling ghost, round as a coin, tells me

of Judas, how he still benedict arnolds
through the meadow bought with ruddy silver:
his neck choking in an argentine knot, his entrails

snaking out like squirrel tails. In His dressing room
like Al Jolson, God masquerades as Night.
He blackens His paint-pink hands. He blackfaces

His clown-white countenance, while a goat
drinks Christ's blood and sprouts fur wings.
A frog drinks Christ's blood and becomes

a green bat. Made of fire, a crackle man jumps
in a thorny bush. He blows me a gas-blue kiss,
then cries, *I am God and you are my new Moses.*

Take a dip? I say, and hopscotch over heat-
baked sand. He pulls up the charred bush
like a tutu, follows me into meringue white waves.

Struwwelpeter: Homage to a Child's Book of Cautionary Tales Dated 1845

The gruesome is an ancient pulse, blooded as a leech;
flamboyant as the barber pole's strips of blood and skin.

Gruesome explains why we open to Cruel Frederick,
vicious boy bitten by the Collie he whips; to Slovenly Peter,

his hair bigger than a haystack, his fingernails more like
builder's spikes. It's like watching a cartoon horror film,

as the Great Red-legg'd Scissor Man severs young
Suck-a-Thumb's best-loved digits like any chainsaw Charlie.

And who can look away from Bad Harriet, a girl cautioned,
who toys with matches and becomes her own pyre?

People love a fire. It's Heinrich Hoffman's world
and the morals are always specific: do not pluck flies' wings.

Do not kill sparrows. Do not stand in storms or dismiss
the brains of rabbits. There is justice here, or sympathy:

two kittens cry pools over the ashes of the burnt girl, too late
to put her out. The beaten dog eats the hobbled boy's dinner,

while the brat, upstairs, swallows a nasty physic
from a green bottle. The sun smiles, looking sharp-edged

as a cut tin Christmas ornament. The hunter gets his,
when the hare, an early Bugs Bunny, steals the man's gun,

and makes him jump headfirst in a well. The hare's shots
shatter a *Hausfrau's* coffee cup, brown liquid splattering

through the air like a comic strip conversation. Like all poets,
I look up at the sky, trip over dogs, fall off a dock into water,

losing my leather notebook. Undersea, I kick up; my shoes
red as fish heads; red as Flying Robert's umbrella—the tin

ribs and silk, the artificial wing—that pulls me out of the sea.
Wind-borne, I'm caught forever in the gilded picture frame

at the end of the book. The storm beneath me sieves blackly
onto my farmhouse. My hat rises higher, like a flying saucer,

and finally gains a life of its own. My hands clutch tight
the umbrella handle, the way a sparrow might guard her wings,
if boys were trying to detach them.

Variations on My Room in the Bone Marrow Unit:
In the Room of Cows

Marc Chagall's peasant is milking a red Jersey cow
incessantly, letting flow a river of cream across
a muddy floor. Here, is a peaceable kingdom of cows,
Danish next to Holstein next to Swiss. The bulls have had
their testosterone lowered with medication and now lie meekly
with the skittish rest of the herd. They no longer bang
their steaming heads against the barn wall when I enter.
The hospital nurse in a cow uniform keeps trying
to tie us into blue gowns, taking advantage of our new
docility. This room is as large as a field but is still
a room. It opens with a double-hinged hospital door.
I sit in a corner, at a drug store soda counter, having
a coffee milkshake. After blessing the cow and coffee bean,
I lace the shake with my latest prescription, a syrup
for mouth sores, a Christmas gift from my pharmacist.
A Holstein serves me, like Elsie in her apron, and a Longhorn
tries to pick me up, but he is easy to resist.
I prefer men, though I know there are other options.
Chagall says hello, but isn't interested in females without hair,
however jewel blue and red my scarf is. After my shake,
I sleep on clean heaped straw. A nurse hooks me up
to an I.V. of chocolate milk, vitamin fortified.
She gossips of great bulls she has known, steamy nights
of alfalfa and Merlot with a Beefmaster in Vegas;
and that recent *ménage à trois* with the Angus brothers
in a pole barn. I make up some travels to India, and a tryst
with a Brahman bull as she checks all my lines:
I.V. tubes flowing in, and Foley catheters running out.

Dachshund Angel

The grey donkey still carries emaciated Donna down the avenue, draped dead over the beast's back like an outlaw. They climb to the beach grass, where fluorescent hail the size of apples knuckles heads, like a child hammering her china doll. My dead dog, Oscar, climbs with his little legs up the telephone pole, a dachshund angel playing violin in his ear—you know the tune Chagall's fiddlers always play. The fiddler is in love, and a spring of Chanel No. 5 flows out of his instrument into Lake Michigan, the fragrance tingeing the water like urine. My father-in-law, inspired by this, pisses into the stream, and afterwards, shows me a guide to mushrooms growing in Mammoth Cave. I look away from his hands and think of Stephen Bishop, the diminutive slave who explored those red clay caverns, smoking his name into the stone ceilings with lanterns; his handiwork now historic graffiti. The donkey and corpse arrive at the cave mouth. They burn down to ash in the sunset and are reborn, astonishingly, as irises. The sky is splendid, the trees covered with pigeon shit, the colors of every berry you've ever seen.

One Hundred and Ten Days

Under this roof of rectangular things: the motorized bed;
electrical outlets; metallic I.V. machines, clicking
and humming—the only things oddly shaped are the people
in the angled-up beds and the round hanging bags
of chemotherapy. The bed-riding person must push
a red button for a nurse to come: *Nurse, I can't breathe.*
Nurse, I have anger. Nurse, let me die. In the bathroom,
where urine is carefully measured, a beaded string
can be pulled for help, the spaced plastic beads like a cheap
childhood rosary. There'd be surprisingly little to watch
from the sky. Nurses run in and out. Patients are patient
or not. Doctors are caring or not (even their hello's
cost seventy-five dollars.) The hallways are oval,
like a high school track. The nurses go on rounds
and wake you with anti-fungal mouth medications,
racks of test tubes and blood pressure cuffs.
The thermometer beeps when it decides your temperature.
You never get used to the way veins constrict
during pressure checks; never get used to the endless line
of needles: blood oxygen pricks on hands, I.V.'s inserted
into arm and chest, blood drawings inside elbows,
huge bone marrow needles in the hip bones.
(You say *next time you stick that stake in me,*
damn well make sure I'm unconscious.) You might as well
be an appliance plugged to the wall, each five days
of chemotherapy. Move, and alarms go off. Unplug yourself;
alarms go off. The chemotherapy drips, clicks, hums
into veins. The anti-nauseas fog you up.
You flip the T.V. channels: try to focus on *Star Trek*,
Barney, Regis and Kathy Lee, then use your hospital tray
for a desk, writing valentines, wedding thank you's,
Christmas cards, on drugs. You recopy your address book,
grade your students' class work, on drugs. Everyone gets an A.

Thirty days in the bone marrow unit and you never leave
the room. You think of Madeline who studied the crack
in her hospital ceiling, the one that looked like a rabbit;
play with the blue paper mask the cleaning girl gives you
when she comes in. You turn the mask into a tent, a bedpan,
a bow tie, a bonnet, a moth, a kidney. You start to order
plain mashed potatoes and cream of wheat for meals.
You could easily starve yourself; put a photo of your family
by the bed. Once a day, the nurse unhooks you
from the I.V. to shower, covers your chest with plastic wrap,
then leaves. You always take longer than you need
in the water—stay under its pulse; rinse off the strange
chemical smells you emit. And after you step out,
drying slowly, and peeling the plastic from under arm
and over nipple, you try to cover the hospital's smell
with baby powder, change to a fresh blue gown.
You could walk to the bed, call the nurse, say, *I'm ready
to be re-hooked now*, but never do. There are whole minutes
when you keep the closed door and walk to every corner
of the room, not connected to anything.

photo by Mary Whalen

Julie Moulds, a Michigan native, grew up in North Muskegon, and earned her B.A. at Hope College. She has taught Children's Literature at several colleges and currently teaches creative writing to kids. She is also the librettist of the operetta *Baba Yaga*, which is based on Russian folk tales. Her poems have appeared in *Cream City Review, Gulf Coast, Marlboro Review, New Millenium Writings, New York Quarterly,* and *Quarterly West.*